Understanding The Language Of Music
A Drummer's Guide To Theory And Harmony

By Ron Spagnardi

Design And Layout By Michele Newhouse

CD Recorded By Butch Jones

Published By
Modern Drummer Publications, Inc.
12 Old Bridge Road
Cedar Grove, NJ 07009 USA

Contents

Introduction

Have you ever noticed how many of the world's most influential drummers have a deeper understanding of music, and some experience on another instrument? Take, for example, the piano skills of Jack DeJohnette and Philly Joe Jones. Then there's Elvin Jones' guitar playing…Joe Morello's early training as a classical violinist…Louie Bellson, Tony Williams, Mike Portnoy and Stewart Copeland's composing and arranging abilities…Phil Collins' and Don Henley's songwriting talents…Max Roach's understanding of theory and harmony, and Alan Dawson's skill on vibes.

Learning a secondary instrument, combined with an understanding of the language of music, will undoubtedly make you a more musical drummer. When you know more about melody, harmony, scales, and chords, you become more of a *total* musician. And as a total musician, you're much more valuable as a drummer in just about any musical situation.

There's really no need to be in the dark when your keyboard player says, "Let's substitute a D♭9 chord for the G7 on the fourth bar of the chorus." Or when your guitarist suggests a I, VI, II, V chord progression at the bridge. If you want to know what's going on around you and contribute to the process of making music, you need to know more than 8th notes on the hi-hat and a snare drum backbeat.

There are many ways to obtain the knowledge you need. Guitar is a great instrument for understanding more about chord progressions. Learning bass can help you understand why your bass player chose a particular line on a tune. However, I've found that a general understanding of a keyboard instrument is the fastest, easiest way to pick up on the basics.

Once you grasp the mechanics of keyboard, it's like having an entire orchestra at your fingertips. Melody, theory, harmony, and chord progressions all come together right there in front of you. The keyboard offers an opportunity to visually and aurally get a handle on scales, voicings, and chord structure. You also learn why certain things work musically and others don't, in accordance with the rules of music that have been handed down. A deeper knowledge can add to your appreciation of different types of music—and have a major influence on how you relate to your bandmates from a musical perspective. And if you've ever had the desire to write or arrange, it can open the door to that as well.

In order to gain maximum benefit from this book, you'll need access to a keyboard instrument. A piano would be the obvious first choice. However, an organ, a synthesizer, or a simple five-octave portable keyboard unit (61 keys) will suffice. It's essential to see, hear, and practice the wealth of information that'll be presented here.

For those who feel they have little time in their schedule to learn another instrument, bear in mind that it's not our purpose to turn you into a virtuoso keyboard player. Helping you to understand the essentials of music theory via the keyboard is our only objective here.

Throughout this book we'll be discussing many things you may have heard of before, but never really understood. We'll be shedding light on key signatures, scales, intervals, inversions, the Roman numeral system, diatonic harmony, chord structure, progressions, voicings, alterations, extensions, and more. We'll start out with the basics and gradually proceed to a more advanced level. Sure, it's a lot to absorb. But it should be no more difficult than when you had to master the double-stroke roll or develop your hand and foot coordination.

In Part 1 we'll begin with keyboard recognition and note names. Study and practice the assignments, and you'll be amazed at how quickly your understanding of theory and harmony will expand. Who knows? Eventually, when your keyboard player calls for that D♭9 chord on the fourth bar of the chorus, not only will you know what he's talking about—you may even be able to suggest an A minor instead!

Ron Spagnardi

Part 1: The Basics

Before we can begin our study of the language of music, we need to have a good understanding of the basics of music notation. So here goes.

Music is notated on a **staff** made up of five lines and four spaces.

Notes are placed on the five lines and within the four spaces.

Vertical **bar lines** separate one group of notes from another on the staff.

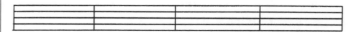

The **treble clef** sign identifies notes above middle C on the keyboard. These notes are most commonly played by the right hand.

The **bass clef** sign identifies notes below middle C on the keyboard. These notes are generally played by the left hand.

Now let's get familiar with the layout of the keyboard. Look at the example below and notice the pattern of white keys spaced between a series of three and then two black keys. Note below how the pattern repeats itself along the keyboard.

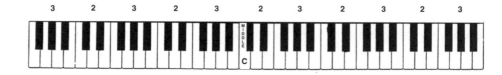

All of the keys on the keyboard are named in relation to the first seven letters of the alphabet: **A B C D E F G**. Every white key can be easily recognized by its position in relation to a black key group.

Notice in the example that follows where the seven lettered notes appear in relation to the black keys.

Here's an entire keyboard that includes the letter names of all the white notes. Notice the repetition up and down the keyboard. Study the layout and be able to identify all of the white notes on the keyboard.

Remember the five lines and four spaces we discussed earlier? Below you'll find all of the notes placed on the treble and bass clefs. Starting with **middle C**, the right-hand treble clef notes move upward in alphabetical sequence (**C, D, E, F, G, A, B, C,** etc.), while the left-hand bass clef notes move downward (**C, B, A, G, F, E, D, C,** etc.).

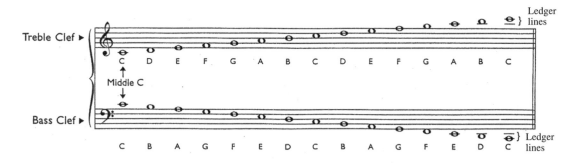

Study the example below to see how the notes on the staff correspond with the keys on the keyboard.

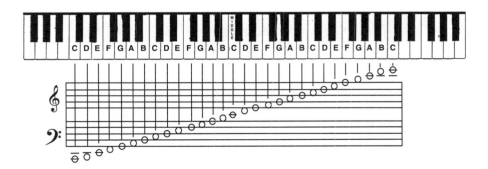

It's essential to familiarize yourself with all the notes on the treble and bass clefs and where they appear on the keyboard. Be sure to spend the time necessary to absorb all of the material above.

Part 2: Accidentals And Intervals

Accidentals are the black notes on your keyboard. An accidental is a symbol that alters the pitch of a note by a half step (to the next available note to the right or left). A **sharp sign (#)** raises the pitch of a note by a half step. Here are the sharp names for the notes on the keyboard and how they would appear on the staff.

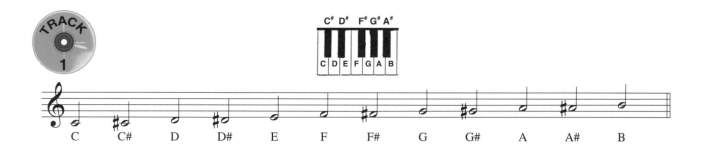

A **flat sign (♭)** *lowers* the pitch of a note by a half step. The following example shows the flat letter names for the black notes and how they would appear on the staff.

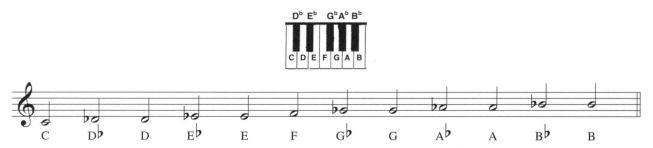

Notice that the black keys have two names and can be called either sharp or flat. C# and D♭ are the same notes on the keyboard. F# and G♭ are also the same notes on the keyboard. Notes that are the same, but have two different names, are called **enharmonics**.

The accidentals in a measure continue to apply until the very end of the measure. A **natural sign (♮)** cancels a sharp or flat. The slate is wiped clean at the beginning of the next measure.

Look at the example below. The flat sign on the B line indicates that all Bs are flatted (beats 1 and 2). The natural sign on the fourth beat *cancels* the B♭ and returns it to a B natural. At the start of the second measure, all Bs revert back to B♭ again.

Intervals

An interval is the distance between two notes. Intervals are made up of **half steps** and **whole steps**, a half step being the shortest distance between two notes. On the keyboard, a half step is the very next note to the right or left. Two half steps equal one whole step.

Let's observe how whole steps and half steps apply to major scales. The formula for any major scale is as follows (W = whole step, H = half step): W, W, H, W, W, W, H.

The example below shows the **C major scale** (C to C, all white keys). Notice how the whole step/half step formula gives us the notes of the C major scale. Try the scale on your keyboard and count the whole steps and half steps as you go. Keep in mind that the same formula works for *every* major scale.

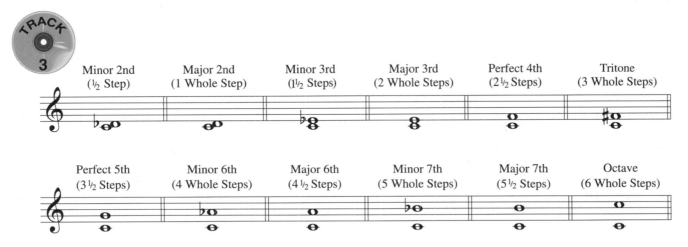

Here's the **G major scale**. Note how the same formula applies, making the next-to-last note an F#.

Once we have a grasp of half steps and whole steps, we can progress to the name of each interval on the keyboard. Below you'll find all the interval names starting from middle C.

Notice how the whole and half steps increase as you move from one interval to the next.

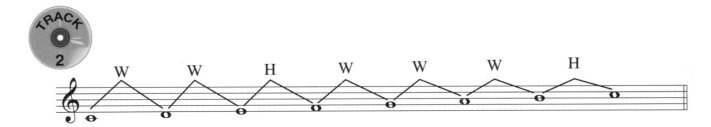

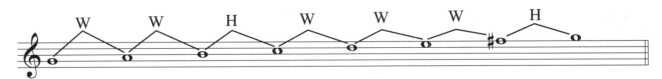

Take the time to review sharps and flats on the keyboard and the staff. Also, memorize the major scale formula and the names of all the intervals in the example above.

In Part 3, we'll cover key signatures along with all the major scales—the building blocks of *everything* that will follow in this book.

Part 3: Key Signatures And Scales

There are twelve major scales in music, one for every note on your keyboard. Every scale has its own key signature, ranging from no sharps or flats (the key of C), up to five sharps (the key of B), and six flats (the key of G♭). The key signature appears at the very beginning of the staff on the lines and spaces. It tells us what notes are played sharp or flat throughout the piece, unless cancelled by a natural sign.

The example below shows the key signatures for each of the twelve major keys.

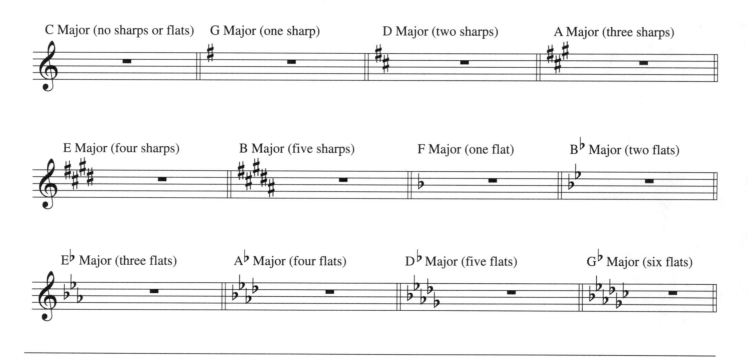

The Twelve Major Scales

The twelve major scales (one octave ascending and descending) appear in the following example. They're the building blocks of everything that will follow. Practice each scale on your keyboard slowly, and try to learn one new one every day.

Keep in mind that the accidentals (sharps and flats) would not normally be written next to each note, as that's already been established by the key signature. We've included them here simply to make it a bit easier for you to learn each scale.

Also, notice the numbers (1 through 8) beneath each note. Every note of an eight-note scale is assigned a number. These are called the scale degrees. Using the C major scale as an example, C is the first degree, D is the second degree, E is the third degree, etc.

Practice all of the twelve major scales. Also pay careful attention to the *scale degree* numbers beneath each note. You'll need to be familiar with them when we move on to basic chord structure in Part 4.

Ascending   Descending

B♭ Major (two flats: B♭ and E♭)

Scale Degree: (1   2   3   4   5   6   7   8)   (8   7   6   5   4   3   2   1)

E♭ Major (three flats: B♭, E♭, and A♭)

Scale Degree: (1   2   3   4   5   6   7   8)   (8   7   6   5   4   3   2   1)

A♭ Major (four flats: B♭, E♭, A♭, and D♭)

Scale Degree: (1   2   3   4   5   6   7   8)   (8   7   6   5   4   3   2   1)

D♭ Major (five flats: B♭, E♭, A♭, D♭, and G♭)

Scale Degree: (1   2   3   4   5   6   7   8)   (8   7   6   5   4   3   2   1)

G♭ Major (six flats: B♭, E♭, A♭, D♭, G♭, and C♭)

Scale Degree: (1   2   3   4   5   6   7   8)   (8   7   6   5   4   3   2   1)

Part 4: Basic Chord Structure

In Part 3 we learned about key signatures and the twelve major scales. Now you'll see why scales are the *foundation* of chord structure. A **chord** can be defined as three or more notes played simultaneously, in harmony with one another. The most basic chord consists of three notes and is called a triad. Triads are built by stacking three notes from a scale. Look at the C major scale below.

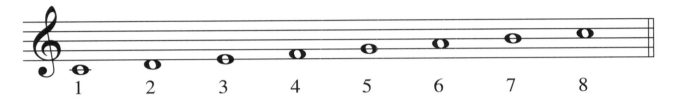

Major Triads

To build a C major triad, we use the *first* degree of the scale, C (also called the root), the *third* degree (E), and the *fifth* degree (G). The three notes played together make up a C major triad.

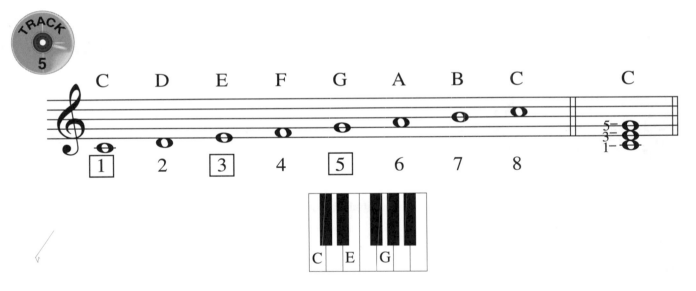

In the next example you'll find the major triads in all twelve keys, each one built on the root, third, and fifth of its scale. Practice and learn them all.

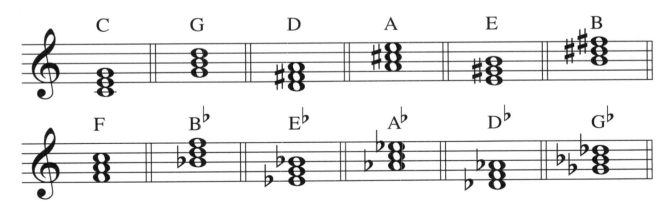

Minor Triads

There are three primary triad alterations, each of which produces a different tonal quality. The first is a minor triad. To build a minor triad, *lower the third* degree of the scale by a half step, leaving the root and fifth the same. The E now becomes an E♭. The symbol for a C minor triad can be either Cm or C-.

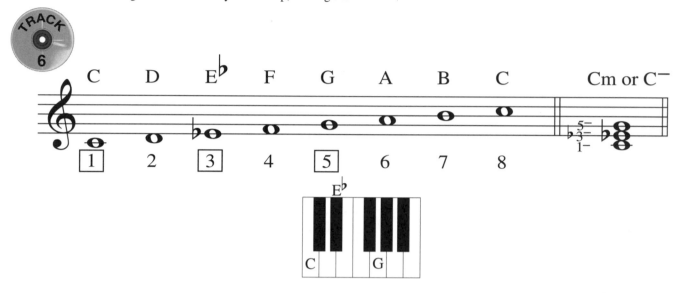

Below you'll find the minor triads in all twelve keys, each one built on the root, lowered third, and fifth of the scale.

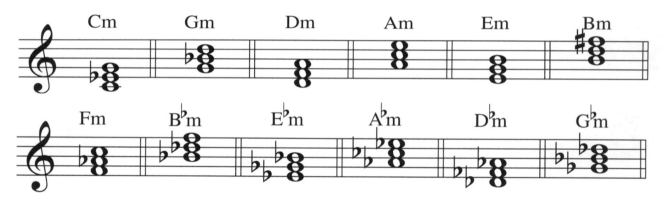

Augmented Triads

To build an augmented triad, *raise* the fifth degree of the scale by a half step, leaving the root and third the same. The G now becomes a G♯. The symbol for a C augmented triad can be Caug or C+.

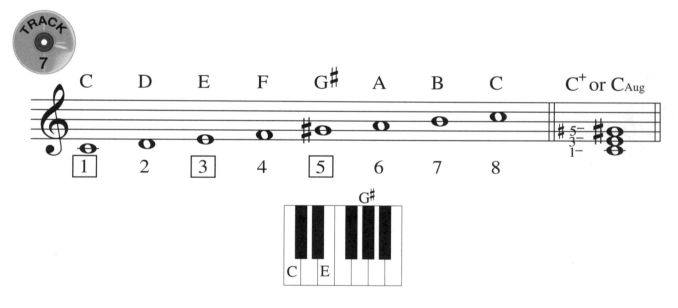

Here are the augmented triads in all twelve keys. (In the B augmented chord, you'll see a "×" indicated before the top note. This symbol is referred to as a double sharp, and means that the note is raised by two half steps. In this particular case the F would be raised to a G.)

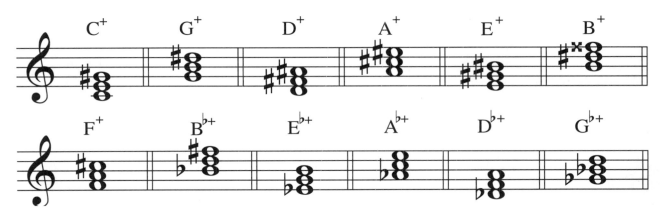

Diminished Triads

Our final alteration is called "diminished." To build a diminished triad, lower the third *and* the fifth degree of the scale by a half step. The E now becomes E♭ and the G becomes G♭. The symbol for a C diminished triad is either Cdim or C°.

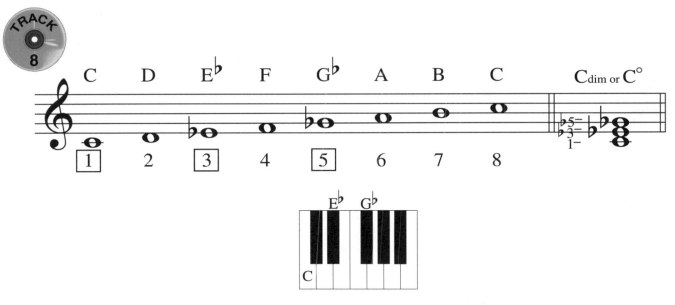

Here are the diminished triads in all twelve keys. Try them all on your keyboard. (You'll notice that within the last four chords there are notes that have two flat signs in front of them. Those notes are to be lowered by two half steps.)

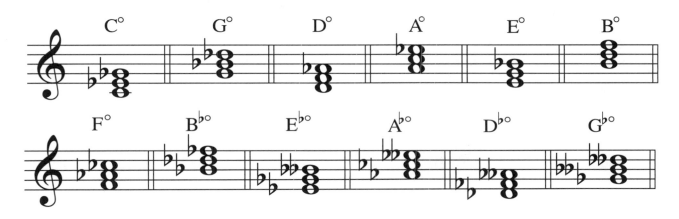

Spend time practicing and learning the four types of triads (major, minor, augmented, and diminished) in every key. In Part 5, we'll learn how triads can be played in several positions, known as *inversions*.

Let's now look at how triads can be inverted (played in different positions) on the keyboard.

An inversion is a chord with a note *other* than the root note on the bottom. Root position is when the note name of the chord is on the bottom. (C is the bottom note of a C triad in root position.)

In the first inversion of a C triad, the 3rd (E) of the chord is placed on the bottom. The 5th and root of the chord move above the 3rd. In the second inversion of a C triad, the 5th (G) becomes the lowest note. Now the root and 3rd move above the 5th.

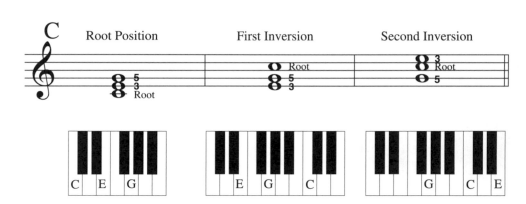

Minor, Augmented, And Diminished Inversions

The minor, augmented, and diminished triads can also be inverted. The following example shows a C minor (notated as Cm), C augmented (C+), and C diminished (C°) triad in root position, first inversion, and second inversion. Try them all on your keyboard.

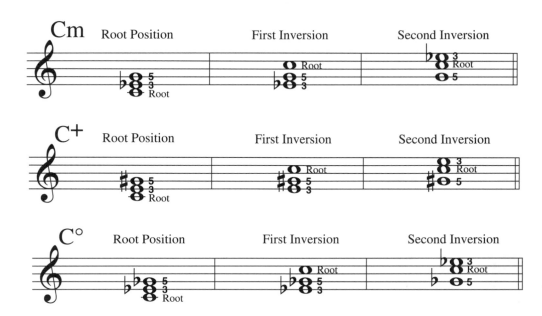

Next you'll find the inversions of the major, minor, augmented, and diminished triads in the remaining eleven keys.

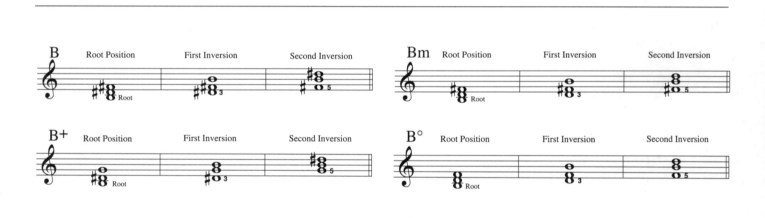

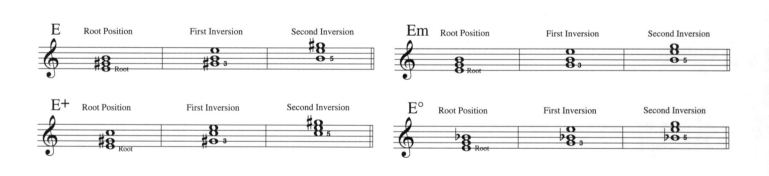

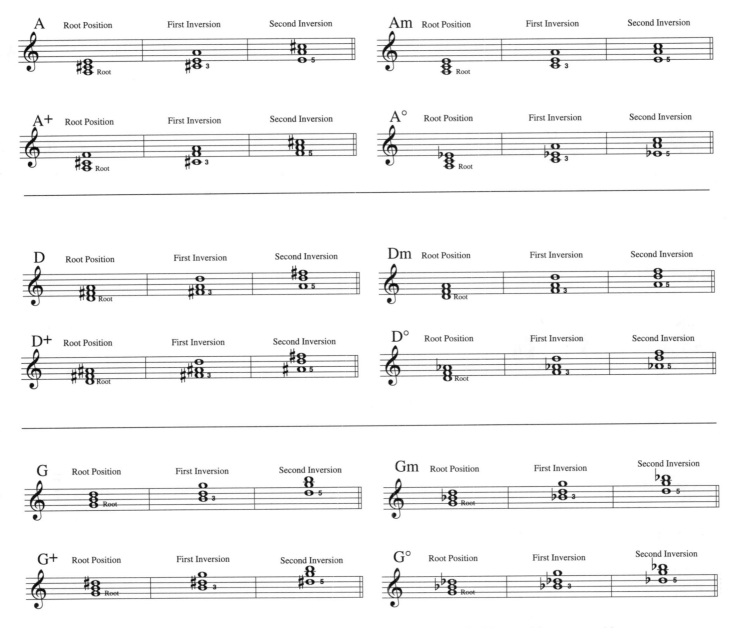

There's a lot to absorb in this chapter, so spend sufficient time familiarizing yourself with everything presented here.

Now we'll look at *adding* more notes to our basic triad, starting with 6th chords.

6th Chords

Triads with the addition of the 6th degree of the scale to the chord are called 6th chords. Look at the C major scale below. When we add the 6th degree of the scale to the triad, we create a C6 chord (1-3-5-6).

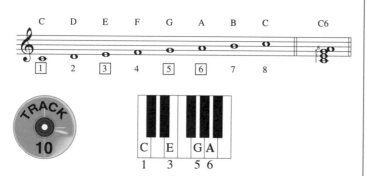

Here are the major 6th chords in every key. Try them all on your keyboard.

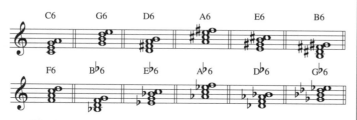

Minor 6th Chords

Like three-note triads, 6th chords can also be minor (1-♭3-5-6). By lowering the 3rd by one half step and adding the 6th, we now have a minor 6th chord. See the examples of Cm6, Fm6, and Gm6 chords below.

Major 7ths

Major 7th chords consist of the basic triad (root, 3rd, and 5th) with the addition of the 7th degree of the scale (1-3-5-7). Look at the following example. Notice that B is the 7th degree of the C major scale. When we add the 7th (B) to the triad, we create a C major 7th chord.

The symbol for a major 7th chord can be CMaj7, CM7, or C△7.

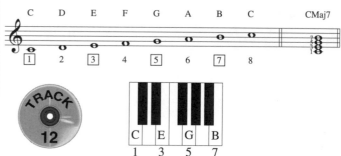

Here are the major 7th chords in all twelve keys.

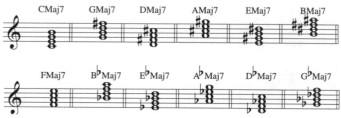

Dominant 7ths

A dominant 7th chord also consists of a major triad (root, 3rd, and 5th), but the 7th degree of the scale is lowered by one half step (1-3-5-♭7). Notice in the example below that B♭ is the lowered 7th of the C scale. The addition of B♭ to our major triad gives us a C dominant 7th chord. The sign for a C dominant 7th chord is simply C7.

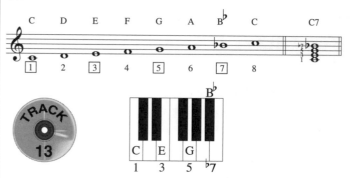

The following example shows the dominant 7th chords in all twelve keys.

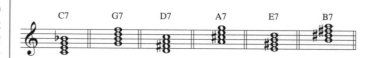

Minor 7ths

A minor 7th chord is simply a minor triad (root, $\flat$3, 5), with the addition of the lowered 7th degree (1- $\flat$3-5- $\flat$7). Minor 7th chords can be written as Cmin7, Cm7, or C-7. Try to find all the minor 7th chords on your keyboard.

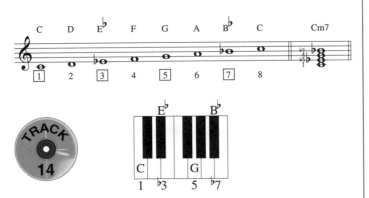

Half-Diminished 7ths

Still another 7th chord alteration is the half-diminished 7th. This chord consists of a diminished triad (root, $\flat$3, $\flat$5), with the lowered 7th added (1- $\flat$3- $\flat$5- $\flat$7). The symbol for a half-diminished 7th can be C$^\varnothing$7, Cm7$\flat$5, or C-7$\flat$5.

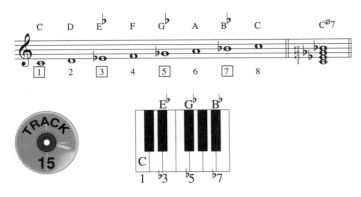

Full-Diminished 7ths

The last alteration on our 7th chord is called full-diminished. The full-diminished chord is also made up of a diminished triad (root, $\flat$3, $\flat$5). However, the 7th degree is now lowered by one whole step (1- $\flat$3- $\flat$5- $\flat\flat$7). In terms of traditional music theory, the 7th degree is flatted twice and referred to as B$\flat\flat$ (double flat).

A much easier way to locate the note is to realize that the full-diminished 7th is the *same* as the 6th. Notice in the example below that in the key of C, the full-diminished 7th (B$\flat\flat$) is actually an A, and A is the 6th degree of the scale.

The symbol for a full-diminished chord is C$^\circ$7, or Cdim7. Try to locate all of the full-diminished 7th chords on your keyboard.

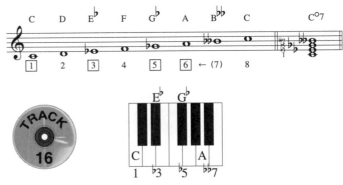

7th Chord Inversions

As with triads, 7th chords can *also* be played in inversions. However, 7th chords will have four positions, since there are four notes in the chord: root position, 1st inversion, 2nd inversion, and 3rd inversion (7th on the bottom). The following example shows a C7 and a Cm7 chord in root position, 1st inversion, 2nd inversion, and 3rd inversion.

For added practice, experiment with all the 7th chords (major, dominant, minor, half-diminished, and full-diminished) in all inversions in every key.

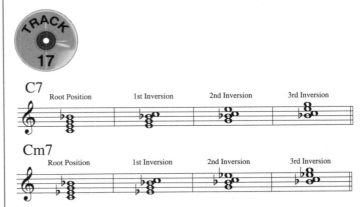

There's quite a bit to absorb here, so take your time and practice daily. Next, we'll look at musical form and structure and why it's essential for drummers to fully understand this important subject.

Part 7: Form And Structure

Let's take a short break from scales and chords to examine another essential aspect of the language of music, known as form and structure. Along with melody, harmony, and rhythm, a musical composition generally fits into a pre-determined form of some sort. Most popular music is written in phrases, and the manner in which those phrases are assembled determines the structure of the piece.

The phrases, most often presented in units of eight bars (though longer and shorter units are also common), are assigned a letter name. The initial eight-bar phrase of a composition is designated as letter A. Other phrases that differ from the A phrase are called B, C, and D respectively. Let's look at some of the more common musical forms.

The AABA Form

The AABA form is one of the most common in music. Here the opening eight-bar phrase is presented in the first A. The same phrase is then repeated (the second A). The following eight-bar phrase is quite different melodically and harmonically from the first two, and is called the B section (also referred to as the bridge or release). Finally, the original eight-bar A section is repeated once again. All four eight-bar phrases equal a common thirty-two-bar, AABA composition.

There are literally hundreds of thirty-two-bar AABA tunes. Duke Ellington's "Satin Doll," Johnny Green's "Body And Soul," Herbie Hancock's "Maiden Voyage," Thelonious Monk's "In Walked Bud," and Billy Strayhorn's "Take The A Train" are just a few based on this form.

Here's a basic outline of a thirty-two-bar, AABA form. Note the repetition of the three A sections (with the exception of a few chord alterations at the conclusion of phrases), and the new harmonic structure of the B phrase.

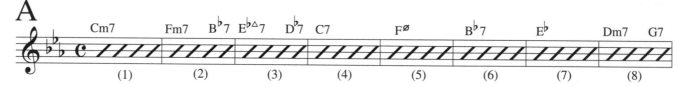

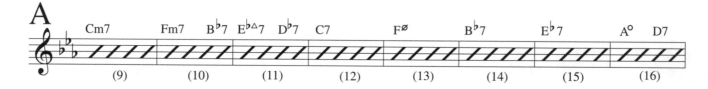

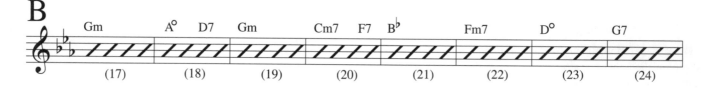

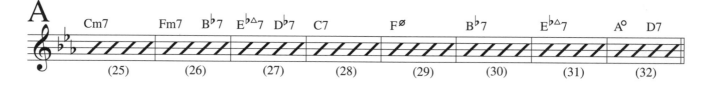

The AABA form can also be an extended version, where each phrase is sixteen bars or longer. Cole Porter's "Love For Sale" is a good example of an extended AABA. Occasionally unorthodox combinations like 8-8-8-12, 12-12-12-12, or 12-12-8-4, as in Richard Rodgers' "Little Girl Blue," are used.

Be aware that not all tunes follow the AABA format. When further phrases are incorporated into the tune, those are generally designated as the C and D sections. Let's examine a few of these.

The ABAC Form

The ABAC structure has *three* distinctly different sections (A, B, and C). Frank Loesser's "If I Were A Bell" and Horace Silver's "Strollin'" are two good examples of ABAC tunes. Here's a sample:

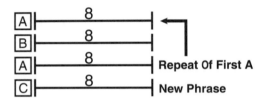

Interestingly, ABAC tunes aren't always thirty-two bars. Jobim's "Desafinado" is written as an ABAC, but with its sixteen-bar A and B sections and twenty-bar C phrase, it has a grand total of sixty-eight bars.

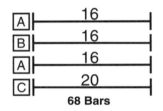

The ABCD Form

Another popular form that uses four totally different sections of melodic and harmonic material is the ABCD structure. A few good examples are Harold Arlen's "Come Rain Or Come Shine" and Ray Henderson's "Bye Bye Blackbird."

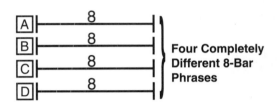

The AABC Form

This structure is unique in that the C phrase, which follows the bridge, is totally different from the previous two As. Cole Porter's "I Concentrate On You" is a good example of an extended AABC format (16-16-16-16).

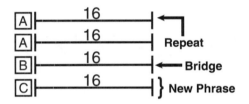

The AAB And ABC Forms

Two other commonly used forms are the AAB (Cole Porter's "Night And Day") and the ABC structure (Joe Zawinul's "Mercy, Mercy, Mercy"). Here again, each phrase may vary in length. Note the extended sixteen-bar structure of Cole Porter's "Night And Day."

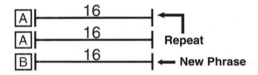

Compare the previous example with Joe Zawinul's "Mercy, Mercy, Mercy," a very concise 8-8-4 within an ABC structure.

The Twelve-Bar Blues

Another common form in both rock and jazz is the twelve-bar blues. The blues format consists of three four-bar phrases with a common harmonic structure (generally all dominant 7th chords).

When a rock or jazz player improvises on a blues chorus, he or she is carefully following a specific chord progression throughout the twelve-bar structure. See the basic twelve-bar blues format below. (We'll be examining blues progressions in greater detail a bit later.)

Verse/Chorus Form

The verse/chorus form has been used extensively for years on hundreds of popular hits. Lyrically speaking, the verse conveys the basic information of the song and serves as a setup to the chorus. The chorus, which is generally the strong, memorable section of the song both lyrically and melodically, focuses on the meaning and essence of the song.

There are many variations of the verse/chorus form, and bar lengths can vary greatly. A few examples are shown below:

1	2	3
A—Verse	A—Chorus	A—Verse
B—Chorus	B—Verse	A—Verse
A—Verse	A—Chorus	B—Chorus
B—Chorus	B—Verse	A—Verse
A—Verse	A—Chorus	B—Chorus
B—Chorus		B—Chorus

As you can see, there are numerous musical forms and form lengths utilized by composers. As a drummer, it's important to always be fully aware of the structure of the tune you're playing and to know where you are within that structure.

Listen carefully to the solos of some of the great drummers, and you'll very often hear the form being stated within the solo. In many cases, you'll even hear the melody of the tune presented rhythmically. Max Roach, Roy Haynes, Joe Morello, and Jack DeJohnette are among the masters at this.

Take time to *really* listen to different types of music, and try to determine the structure of tunes you enjoy. Begin to analyze tunes from song folios, sheet music, and fake books. This is an excellent way to improve your understanding of form and structure. In essence, develop your ability to listen analytically.

Part 8: Roman Numerals And The Circle Of 5ths

The Roman numeral system in music offers an easy method of identifying chords and chord progressions in every key. Here's how it works: The Roman numerals I through VII simply refer to the degrees of a scale. Since there are seven notes in a scale, the first seven Roman numerals are used.

I	II	III	IV	V	VI	VII
1	2	3	4	5	6	7

Look at the C scale below and notice how Roman numerals I through VII relate to each degree of the scale.

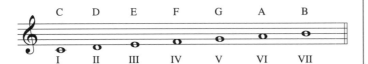

When we build a three-note chord on each degree of the C scale, we end up with the seven diatonic chords in the key of C major. (We'll delve more deeply into the resulting quality of these diatonic chords [major, dominant, minor, and diminished] later.)

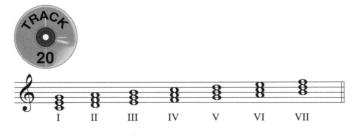

The beauty of the Roman numeral system lies in the fact that it is not limited to any particular key. In other words, the I chord is I in every key, IV is IV in every key, V is V in every key, etc....

Notice in the example below that C, F, and G are the I, IV, and V chords in the key of C. In the key of G major, the I, IV, and V chords are G, C, and D. In the key of F, the I, IV, and V chords become F, B♭, and C.

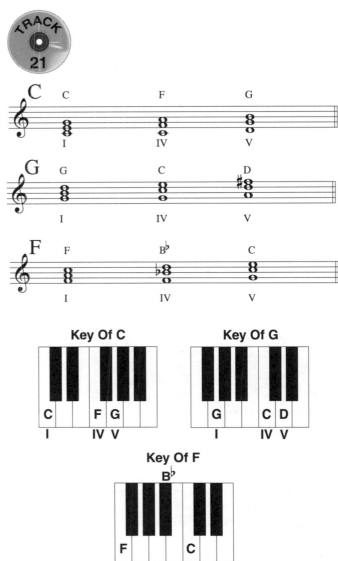

The following chart offers a bird's-eye view of the essential I, IV, and V chords in every key. Try them all on your keyboard.

Key	I	IV	V
C	C (C, E, G)	F (F, A, C)	G (G, B, D)
G	G (G, B, D)	C (C, E, G)	D (D, F#, A)
D	D (D, F#, A)	G (G, B, D)	A (A, C#, E)
A	A (A, C#, E)	D (D, F#,A)	E (E, G#, B)
E	E (E, G#, B)	A (A, C#, E)	B (B, D#, F#)
B	B (B, D#, F#)	E (E, G#, B)	F# (F#, A#, C#)
G♭	G♭ (G♭, B♭, D♭)	B (B, D#, F#)	D♭ (D♭, F, A♭)
D♭	D♭ (D♭, F, A♭)	G♭ (G♭, B♭, D♭)	A♭ (A♭, C, E♭)
A♭	A♭ (A♭, C, E♭)	D♭ (D♭, F, A♭)	E♭ (E♭, G, B♭)
E♭	E♭ (E♭, G, B♭)	A♭ (A♭, C, E♭)	B♭ (B♭, D, F)
B♭	B♭ (B♭, D, F)	E♭ (E♭, G, B♭)	F (F, A, C)
F	F (F, A, C)	B♭ (B♭, D, F)	C (C, E, G)

Not only does the Roman numeral system help us memorize chord changes to different tunes, it's also invaluable in transposition (playing the same tunes in different keys). Once you're adept at converting scale degrees to Roman numerals, transpositions to other keys are quick and easy to make.

The Circle Of 5ths

The Circle Of 5ths diagram on the following page demonstrates chords that move in intervals of a 5th. Look at the example. The arrows indicate that the circle can move clockwise or counter-clockwise. Moving clockwise, the circle moves in intervals of a 5th towards the sharp keys. Each time you move up a 5th, another sharp is added.

As you move counterclockwise, the circle moves in intervals of a 5th downwards towards the flat keys. Each time you move down a 5th, another flat is added.

These natural progressions are very common in rock, pop, and jazz harmony because they are extremely strong chord progressions.

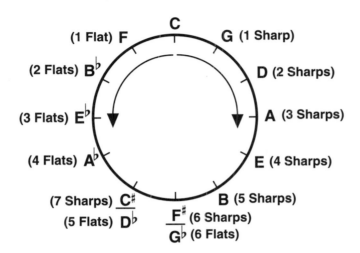

Spend time absorbing all of the material here. Be able to identify the I, IV, and V chords in every key. Then practice the I, IV, V progression clockwise through the Circle Of 5ths.

C, G, D, A, E, B, F#, C#, A♭, E♭, B♭, and F.

Then try the I, IV, V progression counterclockwise through the Circle Of 5ths.

C, F, B♭, E♭, A♭, D♭, G♭, B, E, A, D, and G.

Part 9: Diatonic Harmony

The term diatonic harmony refers to the chords associated with a particular scale or key. The most common way to build these chords is to stack 3rds from each degree of the scale. The example below shows what happens when we stack 3rds and build 7th chords on every note of the C major scale.

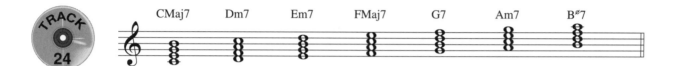

Notice, in the example above, the *type* of chord built on each degree of the scale. The C and F chords are major 7ths. The D, E, and A chords are minor 7ths. The G chord is a dominant 7th. And B is a half-diminished 7th.

Be aware that the chord type (major, minor, dominant, or diminished) *remains the same* in every major key. For example, in the key of B♭, the same chord type pattern occurs. Here the B♭ and E♭ chords are major 7ths. The C, D, and G chords are minor 7ths. The F chord is a dominant 7th, and A is a half-diminished 7th.

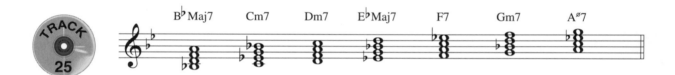

Upper- And Lower-Case Roman Numerals

Now let's bring the Roman numeral system we learned back into the picture. Look at the example below. Notice that *upper-case* Roman numerals are used for the major 7th and dominant 7th chords (I, IV, and V), while *lower-case* numerals are designated for the minor 7th and half-diminished 7th chords (ii, iii, vi, and vii).

I Major	**V Dominant 7th**
ii minor 7th	**vi minor 7th**
iii minor 7th	**vii diminished 7th**
IV Major 7th	

Here's what it looks like when we place Roman numerals beneath the diatonic chords of the C scale.

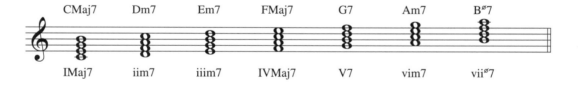

The following are the diatonic 7th chords in each of the twelve major keys. Once again, notice that all the I and IV chords are major 7ths, the ii, iii, and vi chords are minor 7ths, the V chords are dominant, and all the vii chords are half-diminished 7ths. Practice all the chords on the chart in every key.

Key	IMaj7	iim7	iiim7	IVMaj7	V7	vim7	viiø7
C	CMaj7	Dmin7	Emin7	FMaj7	G7	Amin7	Bø7
G	GMaj7	Amin7	Bmin7	CMaj7	D7	Emin7	F#ø7
D	DMaj7	Emin7	F#min7	GMaj7	A7	Bmin7	C#ø7
A	AMaj7	Bmin7	C#min7	DMaj7	E7	F#min7	G#ø7
E	EMaj7	F#min7	G#min7	AMaj7	B7	C#min7	D#ø7
B	BMaj7	C#min7	D#min7	EMaj7	F#7	G#min7	A#ø7
G♭	G♭Maj7	A♭min7	B♭min7	C♭Maj7	D♭7	E♭min7	Fø7
D♭	D♭Maj7	E♭min7	Fmin7	G♭Maj7	A♭7	B♭min7	Cø7
A♭	A♭Maj7	B♭min7	Cmin7	D♭Maj7	E♭7	Fmin7	Gø7
E♭	E♭Maj7	Fmin7	Gmin7	A♭Maj7	B♭7	Cmin7	Dø7
B♭	B♭Maj7	Cmin7	Dmin7	E♭Maj7	F7	Gmin7	Aø7
F	FMaj7	Gmin7	Amin7	B♭Maj7	C7	Dmin7	Eø7

The iim7, V7, IMaj7 Progression

The iim7, V7, IMaj7 is a common chord progression in numerous musical styles, and you should be familiar with it. Let's see what this progression (in root position) would look and sound like in the key of F.

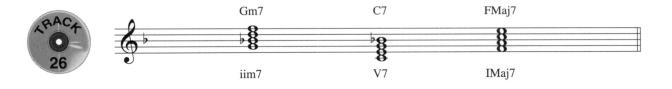

The following is the same progression using *inversions*. Notice the improved sound when notes move in closer proximity to one another, rather then in wide, awkward leaps. This is called smooth voice leading.

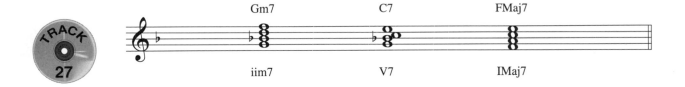

27

The chart below shows the iim7, V7, IMaj7 progression in every key. Practice this often-used progression in all keys.

Key	iim7	V7	IMaj7
C	Dm7	G7	CMaj7
G	Am7	D7	GMaj7
D	Em7	A7	DMaj7
A	Bm7	E7	AMaj7
E	F#m7	B7	EMaj7
B	C#m7	F#7	BMaj7
G♭	A♭m7	D♭7	G♭Maj7
D♭	E♭m7	A♭7	D♭Maj7
A♭	B♭m7	E♭7	A♭Maj7
E♭	Fm7	B♭7	E♭Maj7
B♭	Cm7	F7	B♭Maj7
F	Gm7	C7	FMaj7

Once you've learned the progression in root position in every key, try using inversions of all the chords. Here's a sample of the iim7, V7, IMaj7 progression in the keys of C, G, and B♭ using inversions to achieve smoother voice leading.

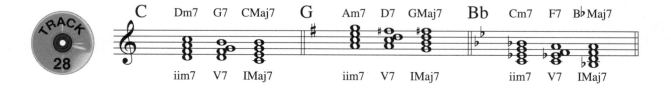

Voice Leading

For the sake of simplicity, we've been notating chords in root position throughout most of this book. Now we'll look further into achieving *smoother* voice leading through the use of inversions.

Look at the ii, V7, I root position progression in B♭ below. Notice how broken up the sound is and how you're forced to jump around when only root position chords are used.

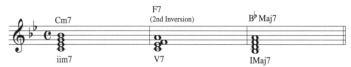

Now look at the same progression, but with the exact same notes in a different position.

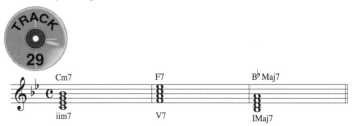

Notice how much smoother the F7 chord in second inversion connects from the Cm7 in the first bar to the B♭ Major7 in the third. To achieve smooth voice leading we need to maintain the common tones in each chord whenever possible, and move notes that must change no further than a major 2nd. (When the hands move in wide gaps across the keyboard, chord progressions will rarely sound smooth or cohesive.) Good voice leading simply means a minimum of movement from one chord to the next.

Here's another example using a iii, vi, ii, V7, I progression in F major. Notice how the common tones are maintained through the use of inversions, while voices that must move stay in close proximity to one another.

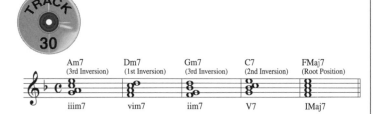

For additional practice, try the ii, V7, I progression in all twelve keys, and focus on achieving the smoothest possible voice leading. The following chart shows the progression in every key.

Key	iim7	V7	IMaj7
C	Dm7	G7	Cmaj7
G	Am7	D7	Gmaj7
D	Em7	A7	Dmaj7
A	Bm7	E7	Amaj7
E	F#m7	B7	Emaj7
B	C#m7	F#7	Bmaj7
F	Gm7	C7	Fmaj7
B♭	Cm7	F7	B♭maj7
E♭	Fm7	B♭7	E♭maj7
A♭	B♭m7	E♭7	A♭maj7
D♭	E♭m7	A♭7	D♭maj7
G♭	A♭m7	D♭7	G♭maj7

The Melodic Lead

Smooth voice leading is also essential when building chords below the melodic line. Here's a sample melody over a iii, vi, ii, V7, I progression in the key of G.

Here's the same melodic line with the notes of the chord progression stacked *beneath* it. Once again, note how inversions aid us in attaining smooth voice leading.

Shell Voicings

The root of any chord is a relatively important note. Both the 3rd and 7th are also essential, as they identify the quality of the chord (major, minor, or dominant). However, the 5th can usually be omitted without sacrificing the quality of the chord.

In shell voicings, the root of the chord is played with the left hand. The right hand plays the 3rd and 7th, while the 5th is omitted. Play the progression below and notice how the quality of the chords are still recognizable without the 5th. Also notice how the 3rd and 7th of each chord alternate position to achieve smooth voice leading.

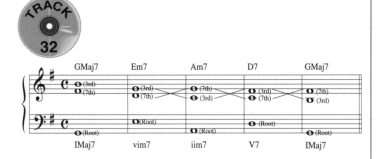

Experiment with the following I, vi, ii, V7, I progression in the keys of C, F, B♭, and E♭. Determine if the top voice is the 3rd or 7th of the chord, and stack a shell voicing beneath it. Play the root of the chord with the left hand, and strive for the smoothest possible voice leading with the right.

Key Of C

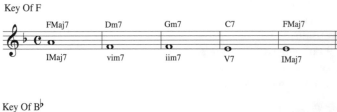

Key Of F

Key Of B♭

Key Of E♭

Part 11: Chord Extensions

The four notes that make up a 7th chord (root, 3rd, 5th, and 7th) aren't the *only* notes that sound good when played with that chord. Chord extensions are notes that are stacked above the 7th for additional variety and color, and are predominant in many standards and jazz harmonies.

Let's begin by examining the C scale below. Notice the scale degrees written beneath each note (1–15). Those notes that fall *above* the octave (9–15) are the chord extensions.

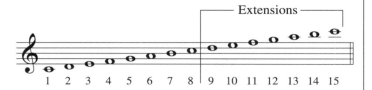

The most commonly used extensions are the 9th, 11th, and 13th. Let's look at each one individually.

The 9th

Notice that the 9th degree of the C scale (D) is actually the same as the 2nd degree, only one octave higher. The symbol for the chord shown below is CMaj9. Chords are generally named by the highest extension in the voicing, in this case the 9th.

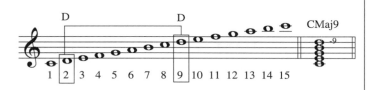

The symbol C9 indicates that the 9th is added to a *dominant 7th chord* with its lowered 7th (root, 3rd, 5th, ♭7th, 9th).

The 11th

Another commonly used extension is the 11th degree of the scale. Note that in the key of C, the 11th (F) is the same as the 4th degree, one octave higher. Also notice that the 9th is included in the chord, unless it's omitted or altered in the chord symbol.

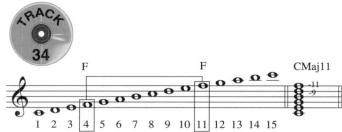

The 13th

In the key of C, the 13th (A) is the same as the 6th degree of the scale, one octave higher. The symbol for a major 13th chord is CMaj13. Here again, the 9th and 11th are included unless they're omitted or altered in the chord symbol.

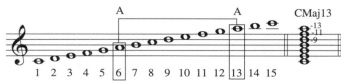

Extensions Quick And Easy

An easy way to locate all three extensions (9th, 11th, and 13th) of any chord is to build a minor triad on the 9th degree of the scale. For example, a C dominant 7th (C, E, G, B♭) in the left hand, with a D minor triad (D, F, A) stacked above it in the right hand, gives you all of the notes of a C13 chord. Try this on your keyboard.

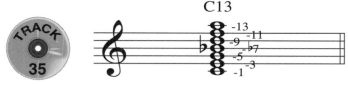

The chart below contains the dominant 7th chords in every key and their extensions. Notice how a minor triad built on the 9th degree produces the 9th, 11th, and 13th extension.

| | | (minor triad) | | |
Chord	Dominant 7th	9th	11th	13th
C13	C E G B♭	D	F	A
G13	G B D F	A	C	E
D13	D F♯ A C	E	G	B
A13	A C♯ E G	B	D	F♯
E13	E G♯ B D	F♯	A	C♯
B13	B D♯ F♯ A	C♯	E	G♯
G♭13	G♭ B♭ D♭ E	A♭	B	E♭
D♭13	D♭ F A♭ B	E♭	G♭	B♭
A♭13	A♭ C E♭ G♭	B♭	D♭	F
E♭13	E♭ G B♭ D♭	F	A♭	C
B♭13	B♭ D F A♭	C	E♭	G
F13	F A C E♭	G	B♭	D

When we alter a chord, we change some of the chord tones and extension notes for more color and tonal variety. Among the most common alterations are the ♭5th, #5th, ♭9th, #9th, #11th, and ♭13th. Let's look at each one individually, using a C7 chord as an example.

The ♭5th And #5th

Look at the two examples below. Example 1A shows a C scale with a lowered 7th, plus a ♭5th (G♭). Example 1B is the same scale with a #5th (G#).

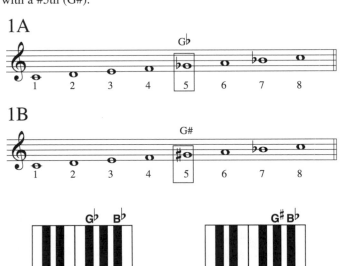

Here are both altered 5ths notated on the staff. The symbol for a ♭5th chord is C7♭5. The symbol for the #5th chord is C7#5.

Next you'll find the ♭5th and #5th chords notated in every key. Try them all on your keyboard.

The ♭9th And #9th

Two other common alterations are the ♭9th and #9th. Example 4A shows the same scale with a ♭9th (D♭). Example 4B has a #9th (D#). Remember, the natural 9th is the same as the 2nd degree of the scale, but an octave higher.

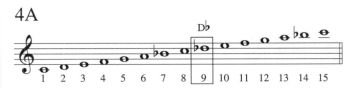

4B

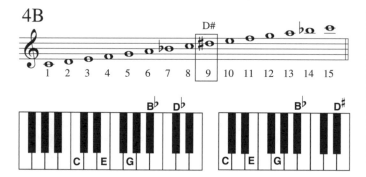

Here are the ♭9th and #9th chords notated on the staff. The symbol for a ♭9th chord is C7♭9. The symbol for a #9th chord is C7#9.

Below you'll find the ♭9th and #9th chords notated on the staff in every key. Play the root, 3rd, 5th, and ♭7th with the left hand, and the ♭9th and #9th with the right.

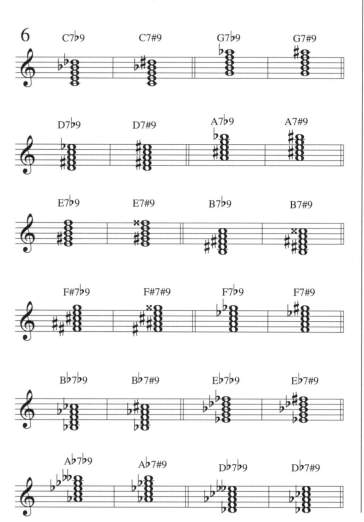

The #11th Chord

The scale below includes a #11th (F#), another altered extension very common in progressive music. Remember, the natural 11th is the same as the 4th degree of the scale, only an octave higher.

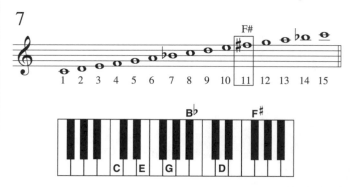

Here's the chord on the staff. The symbol for this chord is C7#11. The natural 9th is included in the chord unless omitted or altered in the symbol. Now try finding the 9th and #11th in every key. Play the root, 3rd, 5th, and ♭7th with the left hand, and the 9th and #11th in the right.

At this point, you've very likely noticed that the #11th and ♭5th are actually the *same note*. These notes are called enharmonic equivalents. Why two designations for the same note? The #11th implies that a natural 5th is *included* in the basic chord. The ♭5th designation tells us that the natural 5th has been *replaced* by the ♭5th. Simply put, the ♭5th is an alteration of the basic chord, while the #11th is an *altered extension*.

The ♭13th

Our final alteration of an extension note is the ♭13th. The following example shows the C scale (with a lowered 7th) and a ♭13th (A♭). The symbol for this chord is C7♭13. The natural 9th and 11th are included unless omitted or altered in the chord symbol.

Remember that the 13th is the same as the 6th degree of the scale, but an octave higher. Experiment with the ♭13th in every key. Here again, play the root, 3rd, 5th, and ♭7th in the left hand, and the 9th, 11th, and ♭13th in the right hand.

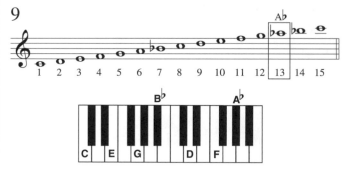

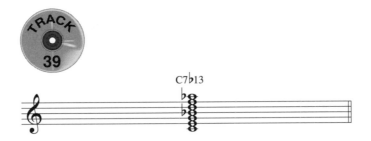

C7♭13

Below you'll find a list of the most common combinations of extension notes and alterations used in modern music, with our C7 chord as an example.

C9	C9♯5
C11	C7♯11
C13	C13♭9
C7♭5	C13♯9
C7♯5	C7♭9♭5
C7♭9	C7♭9♯5
C7♯9	C7♯9♭5
C9♭5	C7♯9♯5

As you can see, there are numerous combinations of altered chords and chords with altered extensions. Spend some time practicing the combinations above in different keys.

Part 13: Chord Progressions 101

Now let's look at some common (and some not-so-common) chord progressions. Some of the progressions we'll examine have been used on popular hit recordings, rock and jazz tunes, solo improvisations, and a number of classic standards. Let's begin by going back a bit before we move forward.

Rock Retrospective

One particular chord progression was the basis behind literally hundreds of '50s and '60s rock tunes, many of which are still performed today. Here's the famous I, vi, IV, V7 progression in the key of C. Try it on your keyboard.

By the mid-'60s, groups like The Beatles started to move away from this overused progression and began to explore new harmonies. Here's a simple example from The Beatles' "Eight Days A Week." (Note, in the second, eighth, and tenth bars, how the customary *minor* ii chord in the key of D (Em) functions as a *dominant 7th* instead (E7), giving the tune a fresh harmonic approach.

The late George Harrison's haunting ten-bar progression on "Something" is also worthy of analysis. Notice in the following example the descending 7ths in bars two and three with the CMaj7 (C, E, G, B) to C7 (C, E, G, B♭) progression, and again in bars seven and eight with the AmMaj7 (A, C, E, G#) to Am7 (A, C, E, G). The descending bass line (F, E, D) is another effective harmonic device used in measures four and five.

Occasionally a composer will request that a specific bass note be played, indicating this through the use of a slash chord. The F slash E (F/E) in bar four is a typical slash chord designation, indicating an F chord with the major 7th (E) in the bass. You'll find more slash chords in measures six (G/B), nine (G/D), and ten (A/E). Notes other than the root in the bass, specified via slash chords, are used to achieve stronger bass lines and smoother voice leading.

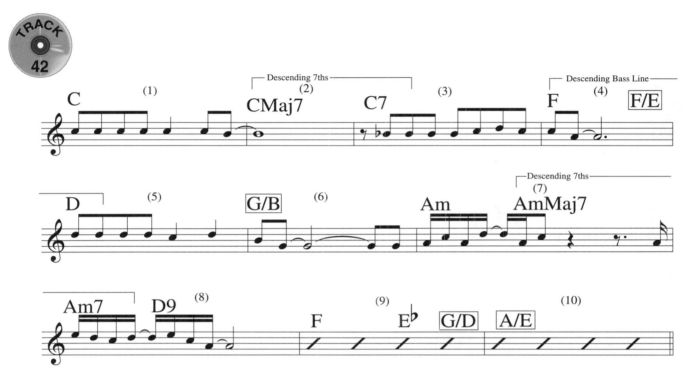

Birth Of The Blues

Rock and jazz musicians have been writing tunes and improvising solos on the twelve-bar blues progression since the early 20th century. The basic blues progression consists of nothing more than all dominant I, IV, and V chords. Here's the progression in the key of B♭. Try it in a few other keys using the Roman numeral system (shown beneath each measure) after you've mastered it in B♭.

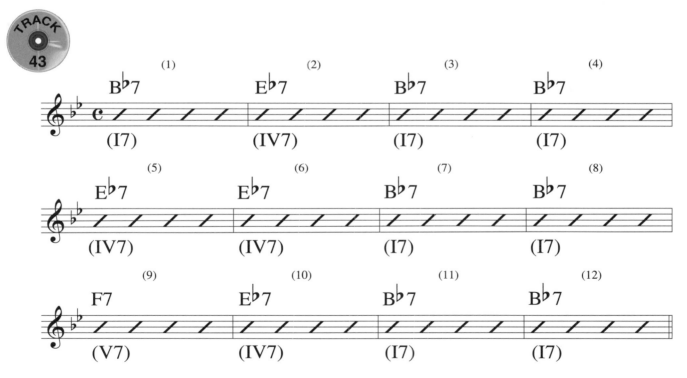

Chord substitution (replacing one chord for another) is common in blues progressions, and over the years musicians have devised hundreds of versions. The next example, common among jazz players, is a much hipper version of the basic blues progression.

Notice how the Roman numerals make it much easier to trans-pose the progression into other keys. Of course, when using the Roman numeral system, it's essential to pay careful attention to the upper- and lower-case spellings that indicate whether the chord is a major 7th or a minor 7th (M = major 7th, m = minor 7th).

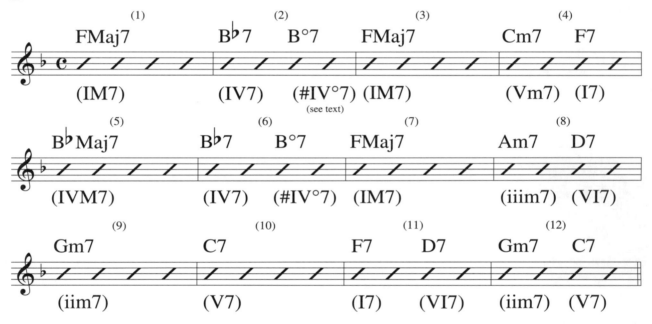

Note: The #IV°7 chord in measure two is not as complicated as it first appears. Take it one step at a time: Since B♭ is the IV chord in the key of F, the root of the #IV chord now becomes B natural. The ° and 7 symbols simply tell us that it's a full-diminished 7th chord. Thus, the chord is spelled B, D, F, G#. Simple!

Let's now examine some chord progressions common to the bebop era and beyond, along with a few standard tune progressions.

The Sound Of Bop

The bop musicians of the '40s wrote dozens of tunes with unique chord progressions. However, the chord changes to George Gershwin's "I Got Rhythm" and Ray Noble's "Cherokee" were the foundation for a number of bop "heads" and solos. The boppers simply constructed new melodic lines over these chord changes. The progressions were fun to play off, and gave modernists like Charlie Parker, Dizzy Gillespie, Miles Davis, and Thelonious Monk, among others, a common set of chord changes on which to improvise. Anything recorded by the above artists (usually available on reissues) is recommended listening.

Here are the progressions to "I Got Rhythm" and "Cherokee."

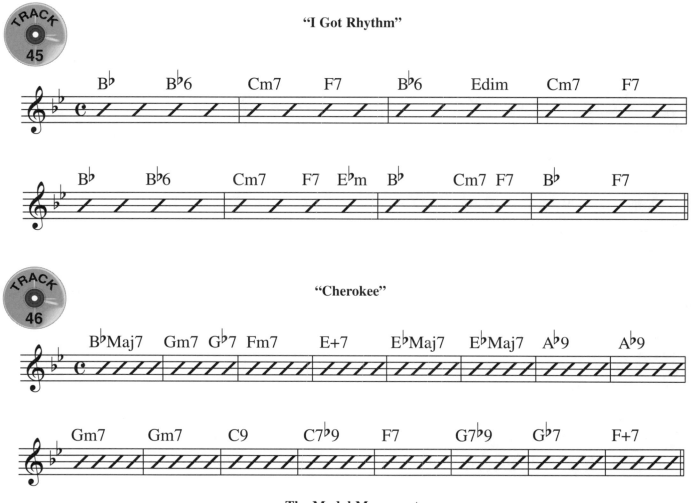

The Modal Movement

The term "modal jazz" gained popularity with the tune "So What" from Miles Davis's 1959 landmark album, *Kind Of Blue*. Eventually John Coltrane, McCoy Tyner, Wayne Shorter, and Chick Corea took the concept to even greater heights.

Modal jazz was based on the principle of very few chord changes, thus leaving a lot of open space for improvisation. The simplicity of the chord structure forced the soloist to focus on melodic invention and the exploration of scales and modes, instead of just "running the changes" as the earlier players had done. Here's Miles' "So What" progression. Note that only *two* chords are used: Dm7 and E♭m7.

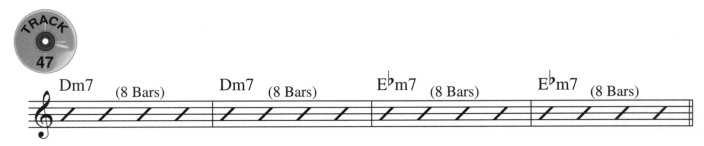

Time-Honored Standards

Hundreds of tunes exist today that have attained the status of "standard." Many of them simply used new melodic lines over basic chord changes, while others were much more adventurous.

Duke Ellington's "Satin Doll" is a good example of a standard tune that starts off on a iim7 in the key of C. Notice the 9th extensions, a classic Ellington trademark.

The opening four bars of "These Foolish Things," containing major 7ths and 9ths, is a good example of a modern use of the common I, vi, ii, V7 progression. Notice in measure two how the 9th of the Fm9 chord functions as the melody note.

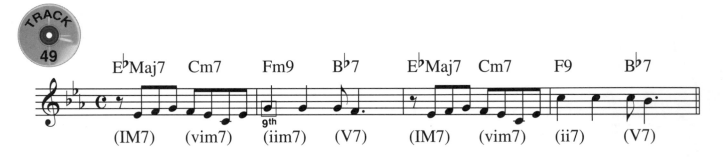

This re-harmonization of Harold Arlen's "Stormy Weather" shows how major 7ths, ♭5ths, ♭9ths, and augmented 7ths could be applied effectively to a standard tune.

Finally, here are the first sixteen bars of Jimmy Van Heusen's "Here's That Rainy Day," a very popular ballad among jazz artists. This version contains a wealth of substitutions, slash chords, extensions, and alterations. Here are a few things to be aware of:

Measure One: The F# bass in the GMaj7/F# chord occurs on the third beat under the sustained GMaj7. The F# is a chromatic passing tone leading to the root of the Fm6 chord in measure two. The slash chord bass notes also occur on the third

beat in measures three and five.

Measure Eight: The #11 extension above the D♭7 chord is a G natural.

Measure Ten: The F+7 is an augmented 7th chord (F, A, C#, E♭).

Measures One Through Six: Notice the strong bass-line movement (achieved through chord roots and slash chords) descending over a full octave in whole and half steps: G, F#, F, E, E♭, D, C, B♭, A, G, F#. A classic touch by a masterful composer.

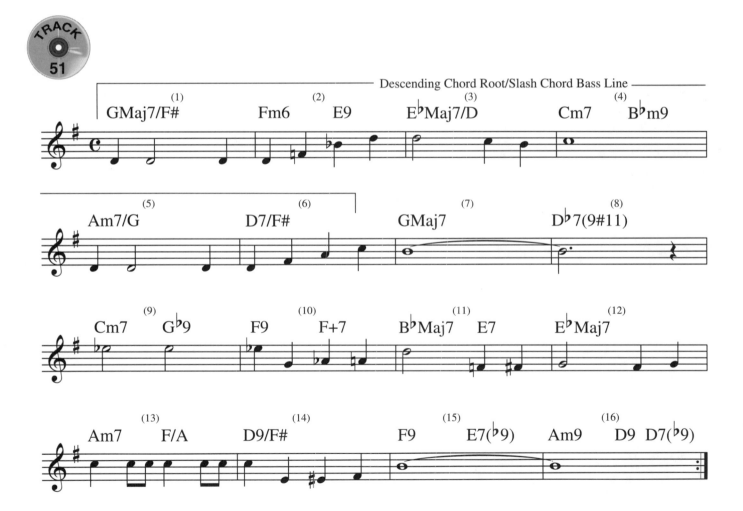

Here we present three standard tunes so that you can test your understanding of everything you've learned, and apply some of your newfound keyboard skills. Each tune is notated in standard "lead sheet" format (melody and chord symbols).

"Time After Time" (Jule Styne)
Key Signature: C. Time Signature: 4/4. Form: Thirty-two-bar ABAC

What To Watch For: Note the I, vi, ii, V7 progression in the first four bars, and the use of half-diminished chords (measure seven) and full-diminished chords (measure twenty-eight). Be sure to always correctly distinguish between the two: ø = half-diminished (♭7), 0 = full-diminished (♭♭7).
 Notice the ♭9th extension (a B♭) on the A7 chord in measure

twelve. Do you also notice that the B♭ on the third beat is the melody note? Composers often make the extension a part of the chord symbol, even though the extension occurs within the melody. A similar thing occurs in measure fifteen, where the D in the melody is actually the #11th of the A♭7#11 chord.

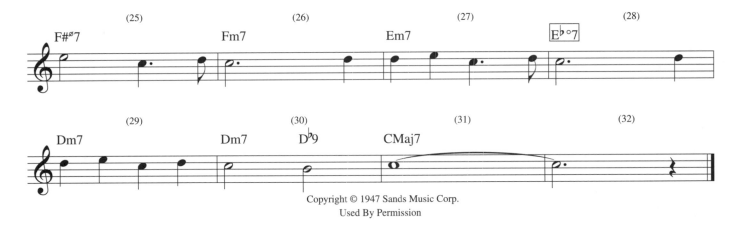

"It Could Happen To You" (Jimmy Van Heusen)
Key Signature: G. Time Signature: 4/4. Form: Thirty-two-bar ABAC

What To Watch For: Lots of major 7ths and dominant 7ths. Also, notice the D7♭9 in measure sixteen, the E+7 in bar 24 (a 7th chord that requires a #5th), and the C-Maj7th in measures ten and twenty-six (a C minor triad with a major 7th: C, E♭, G, B).

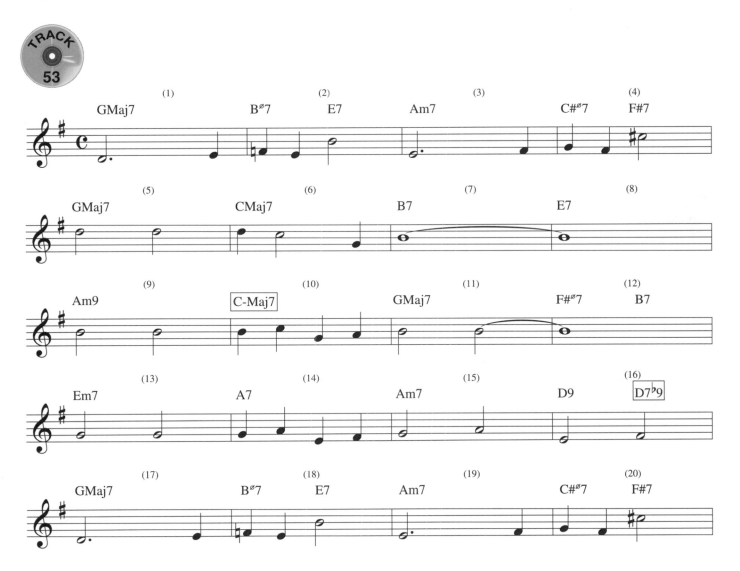

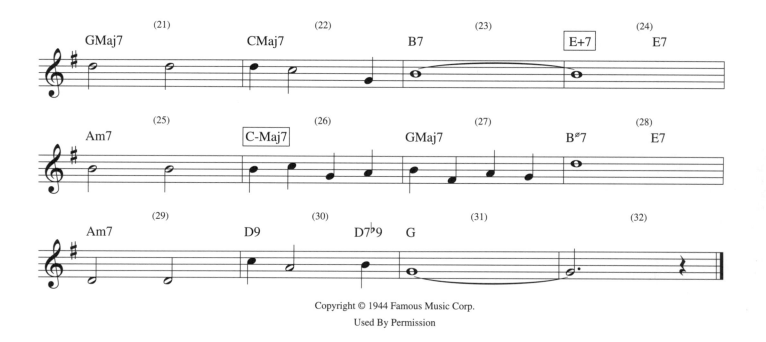

"Come Rain Or Come Shine" (Harold Arlen)
Key Signature: F. Time Signature: 4/4. Form: Thirty-two-bar ABCD

What To Watch For: This great old Harold Arlen standard is the most complex of the three tunes presented. Many non-chord tones are cleverly woven throughout the melody. The chord progression includes a number of dominant 7ths, major 7ths, 9th extensions, and diminished chords.

Finally, notice the smooth movement of the ascending bass line in measures twenty-five through twenty-eight (D, E, F, F#, G, A, B♭). Note how the line gives a strong sense of forward momentum and intensity that builds to the end of the tune.

In case you've forgotten, the D/F# in measure twenty-six is a slash chord (discussed in Part 14), indicating a D chord with the 3rd (F#) in the bass.

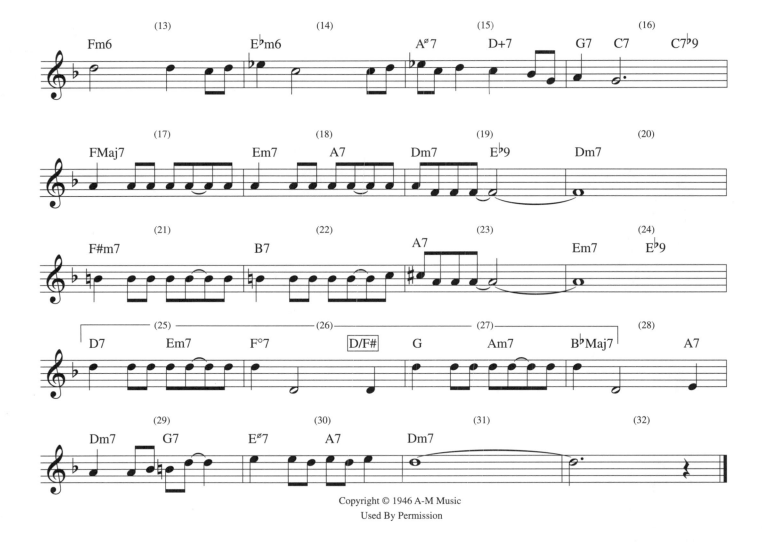

Moving Forward From Here

We've come a long way in this book. Now it's up to you to continue to study, improve your keyboard skills, and further your understanding of the language of music.

Though a great deal of information has been presented, we've only scratched the surface on the subject of theory and harmony. However, there are dozens of great books on the market that go into much greater depth than what we've been able to do here. You can also find a wide selection of song books, artist folios, sheet music, and fake books at most large music shops. This is a great way to analyze the music of many major recording artists, composers, and rock and jazz performers. Don't overlook the opportunity.

If you've followed the book from the onset, you've certainly taken a major step towards better understanding the language of music. Be sure to go back and review anything you're still unsure of, and continue to improve your keyboard skills with daily practice.

As you continue to expand your skills and knowledge, make a conscious effort to listen to as many different types of music as possible. With so much great music out there, avoid getting trapped in just one genre, thereby limiting your understanding and appreciation of so many other styles. As you widen the scope of your listening habits, make it a point to always listen analytically, and do your best to apply what you learn.

Your ultimate goal should be continual growth, not only as a fine drummer, but as a *total musician* with an above-average understanding of the music you're required to perform. The more you know about the complete musical picture, the better drummer you're apt to become. Good luck.

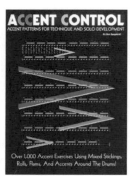

The Great Jazz Drummers
by Ron Spagnardi
60 of the world's legendary jazz drumming greats. CD included.
$19.95

The Drummer's Studio Survival Guide
by Mark Parsons
The definitive book on recording drums, for the novice to professional drummer.
$12.95

Paradiddle Power
by Ron Spagnardi
Developing your technique on the drumset with paradiddle combinations.
$14.95

The Drummer's Time
by Rick Mattingly
A compilation of enlightening conversations with the great drummers of jazz, from Louie Bellson to Tony Williams.
$12.95

Cross-Sticking Studies
by Ron Spagnardi
Dynamic cross-sticking patterns to improve drumset facility.
$12.95

Progressive Independence
by Ron Spagnardi
A comprehensive guide to coordinated independence for jazz drummers.
$12.95

Master Studies
by Joe Morello
The book on hand development and drumstick control.
$12.95

Progressive Independence: Rock
by Ron Spagnardi
163 pages of essential rock and funk drumming techniques.
$14.95

Drumset Control
by Ron Spagnardi
A wide selection of dynamic exercises designed to increase facility on the drumset.
$12.95

The Modern Snare Drummer
by Ron Spagnardi
38 exciting snare drum solos that challenge reading and technical skills.
$12.95

Inside Out
by Billy Ward
Exploring the mental, creative, and artistic aspects of drumming by one of *MD*'s most popular columnists.
$12.95

Double Bass Drumming
by Bobby Rondinelli & Michael Lauren
The most complete text on double bass ever written.
$12.95